SALVATION
THE HEART OF GOD

WRITTEN BY

SALLYANN IPP

DEDICATION

Lord God, with all my heart, I dedicate this book to You, and I pray it will accomplish what You desire. I am so very grateful to each and every person who gave so much of their time and effort to help me bring this book to fruition: including my precious family—Burton, Edward, Patricia, William and Sherril, as well as Bishop E. Bernard Jordan, Pastor Debra Jordan, Prophetess Olimpia Castillo, Pastor Ralph Boyce, Pastor Gloria Boyce, Pastor Flavio Nunes, Pastor Israel Maduro, Pastor Edwin, Pastor Daniel Guerrero, Cathy Adams, Kay Merritt, Robert Mount, Jackie Weatherbee, Linda Glyn Davies, Turner Johnson and Allana Johnson, David Heise, and my dear editor Nancy Arant Williams.

TABLE OF CONTENTS

**Scripture does not limit its message
to any certain group.**

**May you sense the sweet presence of God as He
reveals the true Messiah.**

Romans 10:12 (NIV)
"For there is no difference between Jew and
Gentile—the same Lord is Lord of all and
richly blesses all who call on him."

Proverbs 16:24 (NKJV)
"Pleasant words are like a honeycomb,
sweetness to the soul and health to the bones. "

Psalm 45:1 (NIV)
"My heart is stirred by a noble theme as I
recite my verses for the king; my tongue
is the pen of a skillful writer."

THE CHRIST

Lord Jesus, You are "the Christ," which is defined as *The Anointed One.*

THE ONLY AUTHOR OF LIFE

The true and living God is the only author of life. With great pleasure, He created you and chose to put you here. Before the foundation of the world He made a marvelous and exciting plan for your life filled with everlasting love so dear! If you wonder if God exists, even if you don't believe, inquire of Him with a humble heart and soul, and He will bring you clarity.

Revelation 4:11

"Thou art worthy, O Lord, to receive glory and honour and power: for thou hast created all things, and for thy pleasure they are and were created."

Luke 11:9

"And I say unto you, Ask, and it shall be given you; seek and ye shall find; knock, and it shall be opened unto you.'

Jeremiah 29:13

"And ye shall seek me, and find me, when ye shall search for me with all your heart."

THE ONE TRUE AND LIVING GOD

Father, You are the one true and living God, holy, sovereign, supreme. Because of your great love, You gave the world Jesus, your beloved Son, who willingly came and paid the price, took our place and gave His life, so all could be redeemed.

1 Corinthians 6:20

"For ye are bought with a price."

Colossians 1:14

"In whom we have redemption through his blood, even the forgiveness of sins."

Psalm 71:23

"My lips shall greatly rejoice when I sing unto thee; and my soul, which thou hast redeemed."

GOD'S GIFT OF LOVE

God's gift of love to the world was Jesus, His precious only begotten Son that He gave from times of old to everyone.

Jesus freely came from the holy temple, the holy sanctuary in heaven above, to seek and save that which was lost. For all are His beloved!

John 3:16

"For God so loved the world, that he gave his only begotten Son, that whosoever believeth in him should not perish, but have everlasting life."

Romans 6:23b

"…The gift of God is eternal life through Jesus Christ our Lord."

John 12:47

"For I came not to judge the world, but to save the world."

Luke 19:10

"For the Son of man is come to seek and to save that which was lost."

THE LORD'S LOVE

The Lord loves you each moment of every day, no matter what you think, do or say. He is there to help you always, so give Him thanks and spend some time with Him today.

1 John 4:8

"God is love."

DEAR ONE—I, GOD LOVE YOU

Dear one—I, God, love you profoundly, and you mean everything to Me. Forever, My Word is settled in heaven, for My truth reigns eternally. My plans for you are only good; a life of great purpose have I ordained for thee.

Turn to my precious Son Jesus, for only in Him will you find everlasting peace and security. With a repentant heart, ask Him to forgive all your sins and save you, restore you to life, and set you free.

Trust Him with all—your life, heart and soul and follow in His footsteps continually. Then you will overflow with delight and new hope, as miracles and abundant blessings overtake thee. Dear one, you are our treasure, and our love is upon thee.

Numbers 23:19

"God is not a man, that he should lie; neither the son of man, that he should repent: hath he said, and shall he not do it? or hath he spoken, and shall he not make it good?"

Jeremiah 31:3

"I have loved you with an everlasting love, therefore I have drawn you with lovingkindness."

A GREAT DIVIDE

Father God, your Word says there is a great wall of sin which separates each person from Thee. It goes on to say You have given us free will, and if we choose to do so, we can tear down this wall and come to Thee.

The Bible makes it clear that separation from You is a precarious place to be.

You say that only through Jesus can we be restored to fellowship with Thee.

Therefore Jesus, I ask You to come into my heart, forgive all my sins, be my Savior and Lord, for I long to dwell with You and the Father for eternity.

Wash me thoroughly with your precious and holy blood, for now I realize that soap and water simply cannot cleanse me.

I see that I have been on the wrong path, living the way the world believes and dictates. Rather I need to follow You, the only Righteous One who is able to set me free.

Lord, I trust You and I give You my all—my life, heart and soul, and I give them to You unconditionally.

Thank You, Holy Spirit, for I am being transformed by the renewing of my mind, which brings great enlightenment spiritually.

Dear Jesus, I am blessed as love, hope, peace and joy well up in me. And I delight as I rest securely in your bosom, where I always want to be.

Romans 12:1-2

"I beseech you therefore, brethren, by the mercies of God, that ye present your bodies a living sacrifice, holy, acceptable unto God, which is your reasonable service. And be not conformed to this world: but be ye transformed by the renewing of your mind, that ye may prove what is that good, and acceptable, and perfect, will of God."

THE CLARION CALL

Shh…Listen…What is that wonderful sound? It's a voice like beautiful music saying, "Come to Me, beloved one." Who is speaking? It is I, Jesus. I am calling to everyone with loving kindness and words sweetly profound.

For now is the time to open your ears, your eyes, your heart and soul to Me, while I yet may be found.

You will flourish in my everlasting arms of love, where comfort, peace and joy abound.

Beloved, I am waiting for you with open arms. Come to Me now. Answer My voice, My call, My gentle wooing sound.

Isaiah 55:6

"Seek ye the LORD while he may be found, call ye upon him while he is near."

Psalm 145:18

"The LORD is nigh unto all them that call upon him, to
all that call upon him in truth."

Zephaniah 3:17

"The LORD thy God in the midst of thee is mighty; he
will save, he will rejoice over thee with joy; he will rest in
his love, he will joy over thee with singing."

THE LORD JESUS IS CALLING TO YOU

The Lord Jesus is calling to you, and He has something wonderful to say. He wants to tell you how very much He loves you in every way!

Beloved, open your heart to Jesus, let His arms of love enfold you, where you can forever stay. Answer His call, give Him your all, and your life will be filled with miracles, hope, peace and great joy as you follow Him each day.

Proverbs 8:4

"Unto you, O men, I call."

Psalm 16:11

"Thou wilt show me the path of life: in thy presence is fullness of joy; at thy right hand there are pleasures forevermore."

COME AND DRINK THE SWEET WATER

Come and drink the sweet water from the fountain, the wellspring of glorious everlasting life, a gift from God given with love.

For God so loved the world that with His infinite grace He gave us Jesus, His precious only begotten Son.

You will fall in love with Jesus, who freely gave His life. He gave everything for you. He kept nothing for himself, but gave all He had with profound love and tender mercies so true!

Jesus is calling to you—gently knocking on the door of your heart, waiting for you to invite Him in. He brings the revelation of the only true and living God, which is His good pleasure to give.

Beloved, you will be forever, exceedingly grateful that you opened the door of your heart and invited Him in!

Psalm 36:9

"For with thee is the fountain of life."

SONG: QUENCH YOUR THIRST

Quench your thirst from the wells of salvation. Jesus will draw living water for you there. Take the cup from Him and drink this miraculous water. It is sweet beyond compare.

This unique water brings joyous, abundant, everlasting life, filled with God's marvelous miracles declared.

To find the wells of salvation, call to Jesus, and He will gladly come and take you there!

Blessing, glory and honor be to You, precious Jesus. Thank You for your dear love and care. Only You can offer this priceless, living water so lovingly prepared.

To find the wells of salvation, call to Jesus, and He will gladly come and take you there!

Isaiah 12:3

"Therefore with joy shall ye draw water out of the well of salvation."

Revelation 7:17

"For the Lamb shall lead them unto living fountains o water."

Revelation 22:17

"And the Spirit and the bride say, Come. And let him that heareth say, Come. And let him that is athirst come And whosoever will, let him take the water of life freely."

Psalm 116:13

"I will take the cup of salvation, and call upon the name of the LORD."

TRUST GOD

You may read the Bible and quote Scripture at any time, any day. You worship God, attend services, do good works and pray, merely knowing about Jesus as you go along life's way. But God says you absolutely must know Jesus personally, in order to have ever-lasting peace, joy and security! That's what He wants to convey.

Beloved, make the Lord Jesus your priority this day. Ask Him to come into your heart, be your Savior and Lord, and to forgive all your sins right away.

Dear one, the decision is yours but hurry—don't wait; don't be too late! For preparation must be made in this life for you to hear, "Well done, thou good and faithful servant; enter into the joy of the Lord," when you stand before Him on Judgment Day!

Have faith in God, worship Him in spirit and in truth. Be willing to obey. And with exceeding joy you will hear your name read from the *Lamb's Book of Life*', on that great, momentous day!

Make this your day of salvation. Give Jesus your life, heart and soul. And as you follow in His footsteps, obedience will make you whole.

John 4:24

"God is a Spirit: and they that worship him must worship him in spirit and in truth."

Philippians 2:9-11 (RSV)

"Therefore God has highly exalted him and bestowed on him the name which is above every name, that at the name of Jesus every knee should bow, in heaven and on earth and under the earth, and every tongue confess that Jesus Christ is Lord, to the glory of God the Father."

Matthew 25:21

"His lord said unto him, Well done, thou good and faithful servant: thou hast been faithful over a few things, I will make thee ruler over many things: enter thou into the joy of thy lord."

REVELATION

Why should I spend my life in confusion about God? I have my own opinion, but am I right? It could simply be that He does not exist, that there is no such one as God. But yet, there are so many different religions, so many gods in whom people believe.

Is He just a lie, a goddess, a cruel taskmaster, or an old wives' tale? Is He just a man-made thing like an idol carved from wood? Perhaps man made Him up for his own convenience. Or, is it true what some say— that He really does exist? I want to know the truth, the answer to this mystery.

I'll start by reading the Bible. Let's see:

Romans 10:12 (NIV)

"For there is no difference between Jew and Gentile–the same Lord is Lord of all and richly blesses all who call on him."

2 Timothy 3:16

"All scripture is given by inspiration of God, and is profitable for doctrine, for reproof, for correction, for instruction in righteousness."

1 Corinthians 2:14

"But the natural man receiveth not the things of the Spirit of God: for they are foolishness unto him: neither can he know them, because they are spiritually discerned."

John 1:1-2

"In the beginning was the Word, and the Word was with God, and the Word was God. The same was in the beginning with God."

Deuteronomy 4:39

"Know therefore this day, and consider it in thine heart, that the LORD he is God in heaven above, and upon the earth beneath: ***there is none else.***"
(Emphasis mine)

Isaiah 40:28

"Hast thou not known? hast thou not heard, that the everlasting God, the LORD, the Creator of the ends of the earth, fainteth not, neither is weary? there is no searching of his understanding."

Isaiah 55:8

"For my thoughts are not your thoughts, neither are your ways my ways, saith the LORD."

John 14:6

'Jesus saith unto him, I am the way, the truth, and the life: no man cometh unto the Father, but by me."

Psalm 97:6

"The heavens declare his righteousness, and all the people see his glory."

In my search I've discovered that, unlike other gods, You are a God of love. In fact, it's clear that You love each of us personally.

1 John 4:8

"God is love."

Jeremiah 1:5

"Before I formed thee in the belly I knew thee."

Genesis 1:26

"And God said, Let us make man in our image, after our likeness."

Genesis 2:7

"And the LORD God formed man of the dust of the ground, and breathed into his nostrils the breath of life; and man became a living soul."

Jeremiah 29:11

"For I know the thoughts that I think toward you, saith the LORD, thoughts of peace, and not of evil, to give you an expected end."

And not only are You a loving God, You loved us so much that You even gave your beloved Son to redeem us from the snare of sin, and hell.

John 3:16

"For God so loved the world, that he gave his only begotten Son, that whosoever believeth in him should not perish, but have everlasting life."

Mark 10:45

"For even the Son of man came not to be ministered unto, but to minister, and to give his life a ransom for many."

Revelation 1:5

"Unto him that loved us, and washed us from our sins in his own blood."

John 10:20

"My Father, which gave them (to) me, is greater than all; and no man is able to pluck them out of my Father's hand."
(Emphasis mine)

John 10:27-28

"My sheep hear my voice, and I know them, and they follow me. And I give unto them eternal life; and they shall never perish, neither shall any man pluck them out of my hand."

And what's more remarkable, your greatest desire is to have a personal relationship with each of us as individuals.

Romans 12:2

"And be not conformed to this world: but be ye transformed by the renewing of your mind, that ye may prove what is that good, and acceptable, and perfect, will of God."

God, I have read your Word and it has touched my heart. I am already being transformed by the renewing of my mind.

---

1 Peter 1:15

"But as he which hath called you is holy, so be ye holy in all manner of conversation."

1 Thessalonians 5:22-23

"Abstain from all appearance of evil. And the very God of peace sanctify you wholly; and I pray God your whole spirit and soul and body be preserved blameless unto the coming of our Lord Jesus Christ."

Matthew 6:15 (NIV)

"But if you do not forgive men their sins, your Father will not forgive your sins."

While today it may look like all is well because we're blessed with earthly things like power, money, material goods, and relationships, the truth is that we must heed what You've said—that sin separates man from God. And until we choose to accept the covering of Jesus' shed blood, we can never make peace with You, God.

Help us be mindful that we only have time as long as we live here on earth, to receive your gift of salvation, lest we die in our sins and be separated from You forever. There are no second chances. Forever never ends!

We need to grasp what it means to live a life now and forever without You! This is definitely something to ponder before it's too late!

Psalm 96:5

"For all the gods of the nations are idols."
(Emphasis mine)

Exodus 20:3

"Thou shalt have no other gods before me."

Luke 4:8

"Thou shalt worship the Lord thy God, and him only shalt thou serve."

Joshua 24:15

"Choose you this day whom ye will serve."
(Emphasis mine)

Matthew 12:30

"He that is not with me is against me."
(Emphasis mine)

John 3:18

"He that believeth on him is not condemned: **but he that believeth not is condemned already,** because he hath not believed in the name of the only begotten Son of God."
(Emphasis mine)

There are so many theories as to why You don't exist. We may scoff at the thought that there is a Creator God and think we know better or that we are too intellectual to believe in You. But, in fact, this is a spiritual matter and has absolutely nothing to do with our intelligence. In the end, when all is said and done, we will have only deceived ourselves by rationalizing You away. What a shame!

You have revealed that religion without relationship is an exercise in futility.

---

2 Timothy 3:5 (NET, 2006)

"They will maintain the outward appearance of religion but will have repudiated (rejected) its power."
(Emphasis mine)

Isaiah 64:6

"But we are all as an unclean thing, and all our righteousnesses are as filthy rags."

If we allow it, You will reveal yourself to us.

Therefore, I no longer need to search the world's myriad false doctrines and religions to find the real meaning of life, true peace, happiness and security forever. Clearly, these things are found only in You!

Psalm 139:23-24

"Search me, O God, and know my heart: try me and know my thoughts: And see if there be any wicked way in me, and lead me in the way everlasting."

Psalm 139:1-4 (NIV) (2011)

"You have searched me, LORD, and you know me. You know when I sit and when I rise…You discern my going out and my lying down. You are familiar with all my ways. Before a word is on my tongue, you know it completely."

I do believe your Word and I greatly desire to obey it. So right now, Jesus, I open the door of my heart. Please come in and reside there always. Forgive all my sins. Wash me thoroughly with your precious and holy blood, for now I understand that your blood is the only thing that can cleanse man from his sin. Save me, restore me to life, be my Savior, Messiah, and Lord.

Have mercy upon me. Give me clarity and direction. Take away any deception or confusion that affects me.

Once and for all I take You out of the box I have placed You in. Now I can see that You are infinite—the only living God—the ultimate Truth!

I give You my all—my heart and soul from this day forward. Help me live a life that is pleasing to You. I have decided to always follow in your footsteps. I desire to fulfill and enjoy the amazing destiny You planned for me before the foundation of the world.

It's clear that your bosom is the only safe place to dwell, so enfold me in your warm embrace. And when I stand before You, Lord Jesus, on Judgment Day, I want to hear those beautiful and heartfelt words, "Well done, thou good and faithful servant, enter into the joy of the Lord," and be ushered through heaven's gate, which only the righteous shall enter. *(Ps. 118:20)*

Psalm 23:1-6

"The LORD is my shepherd; I shall not want. He maketh me to lie down in green pastures: he leadeth me beside the still waters. He restoreth my soul: he leadeth me in the paths of righteousness for his name's sake.

Yea, though I walk through the valley of the shadow of death, I will fear no evil: for thou art with me; thy rod and thy staff they comfort me.

Thou preparest a table before me in the presence of mine enemies: thou anointest my head with oil; my cup runneth over.

Surely goodness and mercy shall follow me all the days of my life: and I will dwell in the house of the LORD for ever."

Truly God, You are love!

Lord Jesus, I thank You for the gift of salvation that transformed me and made me brand new.

I will now be baptized in water, which I understand is the outward expression of an inward experience. I will go down into the water that identifies me with your death and burial and will come up out of the water unto your resurrection.

2 Corinthians 5:17

"Therefore if any man be in Christ, he is a new creature; old things are passed away; behold, all things are become new."

Romans 1:16 (NIV)

"I am not ashamed of the gospel (of Christ), because it is the power of God for the salvation of everyone who believes: first for the Jew, then for the Gentile." (Emphasis mine)

Psalm 16:11

"Thou wilt shew me the path of life; in thy presence is fullness of joy, at thy right hand there are pleasures for evermore."

"The blessing of the LORD, it maketh rich, and he addeth no sorrow with it."

Isaiah 33:5-6 (NIV)

"The LORD is exalted, for he dwells on high; he will fill Zion with justice and righteousness. He will be the sure foundation for your times, a rich store of salvation and wisdom and knowledge; the fear of the LORD is the key to this treasure."

Psalm 103:2-5 (RSV)

"Bless the LORD, O my soul, and forget not all his benefits, who forgives all your iniquity, who heals all your diseases, who redeems your life from the Pit, who crowns you with steadfast love and mercy, who satisfies you with good for as long as you live so that your youth is renewed like the eagle's."

Numbers 6:24-26

"The LORD bless thee, and keep thee: The LORD make his face shine upon thee, and be gracious unto thee: The LORD lift up his countenance upon thee, and give thee peace."

Beloved one, if you want to receive God's gift of salvation, say this prayer with an open heart: "Jesus, I receive You as Savior and Lord. Forgive me for all my sins. Help me to seek your face and obey your Word now and always. Amen."

Then you will want to read His Word, the Bible, and get to know Him.

ABOUT THE AUTHOR

Author and Speaker Sallyann Ipp is a multi-talented author, whose works include books: poems, prose, songs and even whimsical children's stories.

Her passion and heart's desire is to bring hope and encouragement to people and to let them know that no matter what, God dearly loves them and has a beautiful plan for their lives.

E-mail: sallyann@sallyannipp.com

Website: sallyannipp.com

Edited by Nancy Arant Williams

Designed by Allana Johnson

www.ingramcontent.com/pod-product-compliance
Lightning Source LLC
Chambersburg PA
CBHW061641130726
47996CB00003B/1404